B
A Life of Love

Zander Wedderburn

Copyright © 2012 Zander Wedderburn

The right of Zander Wedderburn to be identified as the author of this work has been asserted by him in accordance with the Copyright, Design and Patents Act 1988

"Always Marry an April Girl" by Ogden Nash is copyright © 1949 by Ogden Nash renewed. Reprinted by permission of Curtis Brown, Ltd., and permission of Carlton Books for UK.

ISBN 978-1-905916-47-4

Fledgling Press 2012

Printed by Exactaprint, Glasgow

Foreword

B has no memory now, but can still recognise faces. So I started to try to capture my own memories of her, and collect memories of her from other people.

She has had a great life, with her spirit, style, love and charm influencing many others.

I hope I have managed to recapture enough of this to act as some kind of inspiration for others.

The gems are hidden in a necessary biography, but I hope you can find many of them.

Zander Wedderburn
May 2012

Acknowledgements

This little book could not have been written without amazing help from our children and B's friends and family. Some are quoted in the text, and many others talked to me and jogged my own imperfect memory.

Special thanks are due to the staff at Pentland Hill care home, who have looked after B with really loving care for over a year. It is not an easy job, and I really appreciate their skill and intuitive insights, which often go well beyond the call of duty.

The support of my colleagues at Fledgling Press, particularly Clare Cain and Graeme Clarke, has been a huge bonus. They have transformed the presentation and detail of this little book. They multi-task on many fronts all the time, and yet they were willing to apply their skills and pure genius to this little book too.

Thank you all.

Fledgling Press Limited supports the work of Alzheimer Scotland and will donate £1 for each book sold and will make a minimum donation of £100.

Incomplete

I always felt a half
Till I met you.

It seemed like pure grace
When you gave your spirit
Body and all, sweet love,
And I felt whole for the first time.

Now you're not always there
And I ache at your absence
Half there and mostly not.

So when for moments you
Flit and flicker in
Paradise returns

And I feel complete again

Poem written by Zander 2005 for CanYouWrite

Chapter One

Born

B was born in Sussex Cottage, Blue House Lane, Oxted, Surrey, on 5th April 1935, when her father was working at the War Office in London as a Captain in the Royal Engineers. Her birth was registered as Bridget Mary Johnstone five weeks later on 9th May, (which is the day I was born). Strangely her father had been at the Edinburgh Academy at the same time as mine, and there was a tale of them having a fight, which they both won.

She had a big sister Gillian, who was born on 4 April 1933. In those days, there was a tax allowance for a whole year for a child born in the tax year. The cut-off date was 4 April, so Gillian won her parents a whole year of tax allowance, but B was late and missed it.

At some point, I should write the story of her parents, but Norbert Kunisch has already done this well, and Gillian's husband, Michael, is going to expand it one day. He probably doesn't know that a Borders Johnston married a Windram in about 1350, and my mother's mother was a Windram, so that it is just possible that B and I are distantly related. Perhaps a DNA test would establish this (or spoil a lovely myth). At any rate, I never felt complete until I married B.

Soon the Johnstone family went to Hong Kong, from where there are a few tales. She had an Amah, a Chinese nurse. One family story was that she came back from a swimming pool saying "The boys did touch me and I did like it."
They lived in Rose Cottage in Middle Levels (which is now a skyscraper).

It was there that she fell off a wall, where her big sister Gillian had put her, with her little doll's pram, because she thought it was a nice place for her to push it.

They came back to the UK on the last ship through the Suez Canal before it closed during World War 2, with little sister Fenella being born in Hong Kong just before they left. They lived with Granny Wildridge and Auntie Maggie in Henderland Road, Murrayfield, before moving to Bruachan in Broughton as part of wartime evacuation. Little brother Gavin was born in 1941.

About 1946, Mary bought 1 Wester Coates Avenue in an auction: brave woman. B and Gillian and Fenella all went to St Georges School for Girls, where their mother Mary had been Head Girl, and later President of the Old Girls' Association (OGA). B had also been to Broughton School in the Borders, where Mary's brother Gilbert had a farm, Cloverhill.

Chapter Two

Meeting B

My younger sister Susan was in the same class as Fenella, and this kept us apart for a long time. She had a long pigtail that she could sit on at one time, but this passport photo has it off.

When we were 16, both families were on holiday in the Highlands, the Johnstones at Rothiemoon farm in Nethybridge, and the Wedderburns probably at Boat of Garten or Grantown, and a joint family picnic was organised at Bridge of Brown. I shyly sneaked away and shot a rabbit, which I gutted and skinned in a burn while still warm, as my friend Patty had taught me was the best way to do it, and B was impressed.

Later that year, our two schools held a joint debate, where B was impressed by my cocky speaking. Soon afterwards, a joint Scottish Country Dancing Club for the Academy and St George's, called the Reel Club, was started on Saturday nights, and I remember walking B home from it often, pushing my bicycle, or perhaps even giving her a lift in our Morris Minor.

I also took her to the pictures at least once, the most memorable being to Bunuel's "Los Olvidados", "The Forgotten Ones", translated as "The Young and the Damned," a violent tale of delinquent youth in Mexico. B's father came out as we queued to get in, and I was severely reprimanded. We felt it was unfair that it was OK for him to see it, but not for us.

Chapter Three

Waiting
A biblical seven year apprenticeship

B did well at school, and had enough Highers to go to University, in spite of going into her Geometry exam after last minute revision of Algebra, or something similar. But she had decided to train as a nurse, perhaps after her mother's illness with TB, and meeting Pat Ingram, a St Thomas's nurse, in Switzerland.

She also excelled at Sports, and was Captain of Hockey, and even happier playing lacrosse. I once went to watch her playing lacrosse against St Leonards, and she was miffed to learn I partly went to watch Sheila Nicholson in the St Leonards team. She also won the 100 yards, and held the school record for a few years – running in gym shoes, before ladies wore spikes. She also played in the school tennis team. She jumped off a desk and broke her wrist at some point. I think she has broken her wrist twice since, so perhaps it became a continuing weakness.

There is much more B would remember about St Georges – the names and characters of the teachers, from FK to Tatty Thomson to Miss Drever and the PE teacher in particular. B was brilliant at handstands and cartwheels.

Christmas holidays in Edinburgh in those days were filled with charity balls, where you wrote your dance partners into a little programme booklet, and danced to Cam Robbie's Band. I remember B was cross with her mother for inviting me to partner her to one of these balls, although I didn't know of her crossness at the time, thank goodness.

We both left school in 1953, and B went to Grenoble to do intensive French, (which her mother and Gillian had done there before her). She had her appendix taken out there, which cut short her skiing and dancing exploits. I had gone into the Royal Navy on National Service, and we wrote regularly to each other. She was a brilliant letter writer. And she attracted admiring photographers in Grenoble too.

B went on to train as a nurse at St Thomas Hospital in London in 1954.

I drove up the 120 miles from my ship in Portland harbour in a battered 1931 Austin 7, and took her to Covent Garden, and to Irma La Douce. She lived (after preliminary training school in Hydestile, near Guildford) at first in the Nurses' Home on Cheyne Walk near Chelsea, and later in a flat in Warwick Square with Sheila Moore nèe Campbell and Pat Barker, nèe Rhodes and some others.

There is a tale that B sometimes finished putting on her uniform in the bus on the way to the hospital from Cheyne Walk – a hospital bus, not a public bus, but it was still a bit of tight timing. And, of course, a complicated uniform.

I also wrote her a soppy letter from my all-male ship, and she slapped me down firmly, telling me not to spoil things. She was playing the field, mainly medical students like John Restall and Stephen Elkington, but also Robin Croall of the FO, and a young accountant, Ian Tegner. She went to night clubs and balls, and when I started at Exeter College, Oxford, in 1955, she came happily to our Hilary Term and Commem Balls. There are some lovely pictures of these.

At one of the Balls, we went punting in the early dawn, and I fell into the river in full evening dress (I later punted for Oxford's Charon club in the race against Cambridge, for which previous falling in was a necessary qualification). B bravely danced me round the dance floor when we got back, leaving a slimy trail.

My one serious error was to invite her to the Oxford Cambridge Rugby Ball in December in London, before I had bought a ticket, and then, horror of horrors, these had run out. I took her to a Transport Cafe instead. She had some lovely photos taken in London too, and people said she looked a bit like Audrey Hepburn or Princess Margaret.

I think she let me hold her hand to cross a road once, but we never kissed. We used to exchange information about our love lives, like brother and sister, and got to know each other well. I was also a very good friend of Mary, her mother, who loved arguing about politics and ideas.

Mary let B go with me on a 3-day walk across Mull from Craignure to Fionnaphort, and then to Iona where we camped in Dougie Black's barn, to the mutterings of Iona community members. We could not have been more proper – I went out to study the stars while she dressed for bed. Mary's friend, (Rosyth Admiral Luce's wife) said nobody would marry B after that, but Mary trusted B and me.

Chapter Four

Engaging

B went on from St Thomas's to Mill Road Maternity Hospital, Cambridge to do Part 1 of her Midwifery training. At the end of my last term at Oxford in 1959, I went up to a Student Christian Movement conference at Swanwick in Derbyshire, and on the way back I interrogated a college chaplain in the car about how you could tell if you were really in love. His answer, ultimately, was when you wanted the happiness of your beloved more than your own, which is not a bad test, but easier to think about than to do.

I took B for a day's punting on the Cam – I think I was staying with Ray Logan, her best friend at school. We spent a long summer day revising questions from Maggie Miles' Textbook of Midwifery, as she had her exams. coming up. I can still remember what a Prague Seizure is (roughly). At some point towards the end of the day, I asked her when we should get married. She insists I never proposed properly. So I asked her for a kiss, and she said "After you've asked my father."

We took the punt back late, found a phone box, and phoned him. She was a beautiful kisser, always, and that was the first of millions.

B went for Part 2 of her midwifery, the community six months, to Rotten Row Hospital in Glasgow, and I went off to Corby to start as a management trainee with Stewarts & Lloyds, steel tubemakers. We phoned a lot, and I remember a kind operator who let us burble on well after my coins had run out.

My sister Kirstie was working as a teacher in the Gorbals, and remembers B dropping in after an all-night delivery in a single end there. (Single end was a one bedroom flat, with the bed usually built into the wall.)

She was rebuked by Granny for coming down to see me in Corby one weekend instead of spending maximum time with her Mum. She also took the bride's course at Atholl Crescent Domestic Science School, and learnt how to cook cabbage, and poach an egg. We also spent some time touring friends and relations.

I remember Ros Bailey was struck by B's habit of going barefoot. She wrote recently "You had just driven up from London, as I recall, and she walked up the garden path in bare - dirty - feet. It's had a lasting impression on me. Needless to say, we were all won over immediately.

"I also recall that you felt it your duty, as co-President of my Fun Club, to ask my permission (I think I was 10) to marry her! I have no regrets about giving it."

Chapter Five

Wedding

We were married on 18th June 1960 in St George's West, Edinburgh, by the resident minister, Murdo Ewan Macdonald, and Raymond Bailey, who had been my Presbyterian minister in Oxford, and now had a new church extension charge in Niddrie in East Edinburgh.

The evening before, when David Gracie and Willie Prosser were supposed to be taking me out for a stag night, we collected B too and climbed Arthur's Seat, from where we could look down on Prestonfield House, shaped like the Ace of Clubs, with the marquee for our reception in the garden.

I remember acute nerves on the morning of the day, but nothing like when B came up the aisle on the arm of her father, with her bouquet shaking wildly and making a noisy rustle.

I remember Mary Johnstone getting cross with the photographer on the steps of the church, as she hadn't wanted the photos done that way.

I remember an amazingly happy reception, with Grandfather Jeans there, and lots of friends and relations from everywhere. There is a cine film of it, to jog my memory.

I remember in my toast to the bridesmaids, who included Gillian and Fenella, saying that I didn't mind which Johnstone daughter I married, which was slightly over-icing the cake.

Then Gavin drove us off to Glasgow airport, to fly to Dublin.

Chapter Six

Honeymoon

We hired a Mini at Dublin airport and drove into the centre, to the Russell Hotel (which has since vanished.) Over dinner, B interrogated me about former girlfriends, and gave me a rough time over what was an excellent meal otherwise. Going to bed, I went off to a bathroom down the corridor to allow her to change, which impressed her. We didn't know what to do in bed, but we managed.

Next day, we drove down to Tahilla Cove Hotel in Kerry. Our room was in a jutting out square extension, and I think was fairly visible from three sides. Mary had holidayed there and asked the owners to keep quiet about it being our honeymoon, which I think had the result of them doing the exact opposite.

It was a lovely peaceful place, on the shore, and we swam a lot, diving from a rock. B had taught me to dive. (Before that, I was never sure the water would be there, so dived with my face up, with obviously disastrous results.) The food was great: loads of fish and local seafood. I ruined my Gaelic coffee by stirring it vigorously, after the cream had been carefully poured to float on top.

We had lovely romantic outdoor times, going for walks in the countryside and out on a rowing boat. A sheep tick attached itself tightly to me on one occasion, and kind B removed it. Good to have married a nurse.

We drove round the Dingle peninsula in a cross mood one foggy day, and the cool was broken when we drove through a large cowpat which splattered across the windscreen.

There was a 3-year old toddler son of the owners playing in the garden of Tahilla Cove, and when we went back many years later, he had become the owner.

We went for the second week to an inland place, recommended by a friend, Sam, where the window didn't fit well and the wind blew through vigorously. There was a shrine to some saint and the girl at the petrol station, where we bought ice cream, asked us if we'd come to pray. We didn't stay long there.

We also went to Youghal sands. And then back to Dublin and home.

Chapter Seven

Corby

Back down to Corby, where we stayed in the Raven Hotel for the weekend, and had breakfast on a silver salver, until we moved in to the house that was to be ours: 14 Hove Street. The Development Corporation (which controlled rented housing in the New Town bit) would not allocate a house until we were actually married.

Hamish and Hazel Murison were living In the house we were going to have. He was an architect with the Dev Corp, and was moving to a job in Coventry, and he and Hazel took us as lodgers for a couple of weeks.

It was a very tough time for B, as she hadn't got anything much to do. Hamish sold us fittings, including the curtain rings, priced to the nearest penny.

When they moved out, we slept on a wire-framed camp bed, for a couple of nights until our furniture arrived. I remember how annoying it was to have no chairs.

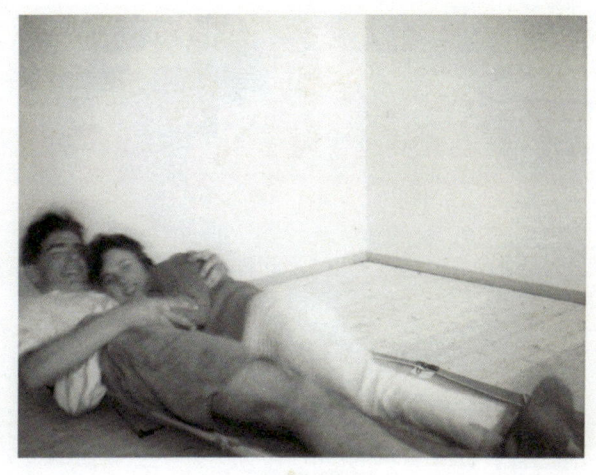

We did a fair amount of painting to the house, and digging in the garden, which was very heavy clay, and had lovely Peace roses in the front.

B was a bit lonely, in a strange town with a strange background. When iron ore was found nearby in Northamptonshire in the 1930s, Stewarts and Lloyds had shipped a workforce down from Bellshill, and built a company town on to a tiny village. There was a bus from Corby to Bellshill every weekend. It became an official New Town in the 1950s, and was expanded and developed prettily by the Development Corporation. It also absorbed DPs, (Displaced Persons) from Latvia, Lithuania and Estonia, so had an unusual population, mostly with Scottish accents.

One of our near neighbours was Wayne Stumme, an American Lutheran pastor, who had come to the Latvian Lutheran church as its first English-speaking minister, because the next generation of Latvians spoke more English than Latvian. The Church of Scotland in Corby was ultra-Scottish, and Wayne had had a postgraduate year at St Andrews. He and Carol had two young children, and B and Carol became close friends. We used to take Christopher to their church, feeding him raisins to keep him quiet.

B also played the piano in church very memorably one Easter Sunday: I still can't hear "Jesus Christ is risen today, Alleluia" without remembering the trouble she had keeping it steady and regular.

Carol taught her how to make scalloped curtains, and how to cook brownies and upside down cake and tuna and noodles. Carol later became a minister too, and we still exchange Christmas cards.

Fenella visited us in Corby, and was wonderful with little Christopher.

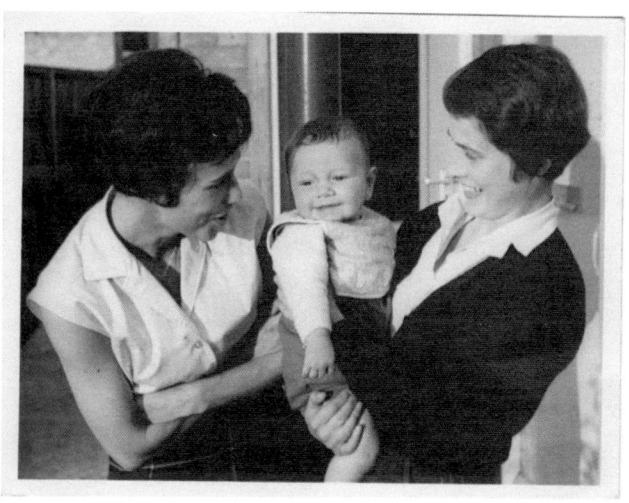

We also became a home from home for Brian Tanner, Richard Phillips and Margie Latimer-Jones. B had, and always kept, an amazing gift of making people welcome, and our house was often full of people. We also went to the Rockingham Arms with them, and for meals out in Kettering. My cousins, Allan, Robert and Christopher Jeans, used to come for a day out from Uppingham School sometimes.

Margie remembers: "When I think of B I see soft blue denim and French navy and the very, very occasional white daisy on a collar or cuff. I think of a woman with a huge heart, who saw the best in everyone and every situation, who was empathic, sometimes very competitive, someone who was warm and funny.

"She took me into her home as a single and lonely young woman and let me be part of her family life in Corby. I learnt such a lot from her about babies and toddlers which I think made me a far more tolerant Mum than I might otherwise have been. I learned about other sorts of cooking – different to my mother's limited repertoire, especially the joys of home-made soup! We all have memories of special holidays in Scotland and their wonderful start. Mike and I had driven through the night with our young children asleep in the back – to arrive at Braeside for breakfast and then to be packed off to bed while B took her four and our three children off for a few hours so that Mike and I could get some sleep.

"I remember all the kitchens full of photos and postcards, smelling of herbs and home cooking, but most of all I remember a loving and understanding friend."

Just down the road from us, another St Thomas' nurse, Sita and her civil engineer husband Brian Piggott lived. She was a beautiful Indian – still is. He worked for Shanks and McEwan, who handled steel scrap I think.

Another two good friends in Corby were Josephine and Maurice Shutler. He was a big brain on the Operational Research side. We've lost touch since Josephine died.

B didn't get a job as a midwife before she became pregnant, and 11 months after we were married, we had Christopher, with a home birth on the night of the FA Cup Final.

I was standing as a Labour Party candidate for the Beanfield ward, and was elected to the Urban District Council just after he was born. I was also sent to night school at the Tec to take an Ordinary National Certificate in Mechanical Engineering, so B had a lot of time to kill. Christopher absorbed a fair amount of that time, and she was a lovely mother.

Across the road from us were the Esplins, Molly and George, and their three girls, Jean, Helen and Mary, who loved to help bath Chris, and they later moved to Cardiff before we did.

Another star pair in Corby were the Hall-Turners. He was the GP, and his wife Yvonne ran the Guides and other uplifting organisations.

A year and a half later, in 1962, Peter came along, and put Chris's nose out of joint. Peter was born in the new maternity unit in Corby, which needed customers.

It didn't really make medical sense to have babies 1, 3, and 4 at home, but not Number 2. In fact, it should have been the exact opposite. But luckily B was very good at having babies.

I remember one day when we were woken by Peter crying, and Chris had climbed into his cot and was sitting on his chest, generating noise.

In 1963, after four years in Corby, I asked what my prospects were, and as a Labour councillor working for a Conservative company, it was clear that they were nil. So I applied for a research job about steel industry trade unions in Cardiff and got it.

For several weeks I stayed with the Esplins in Cardiff and came home at weekends, until we found a semi-detached in Rhiwbina and bought it on a bank overdraft for £3,200. 20 Lon-y-rhyd.

B adapted brilliantly to being the mother of babies and toddlers, and began her cooking expertise in Corby.

Her cousin Mary remembers a visit to Corby.

"B decided she was going to make me a dirndl skirt – possibly I was admiring one she had on and found that she'd made it herself. Anyway, I well remember the delightful blue-patterned skirt she made me, and it was a treasured possession for several years. She was such a perfectionist! (self-confessed).

"Another memory I have is of her showing me how she prepared garlic i.e. I said did she not have a garlic press? Oh no, couldn't be bothered with one of those, much better just to slice it up very thinly. Which she did, with great care and a sharp knife.

I've always felt loved and cherished by B, every time I've come back over the Pond."

Chapter Eight

Cardiff 1963 to 1968

I was hired to work under Ken Jones on a project about how trade unions responded to technological change. Michael Fogarty held the Montague Burton chair in Industrial Relations, and ran the department by travelling from Oxford, for two days a week. He wrote a book a year on books he had read, with a Christian Democrat/Liberal party slant. George Thomason ran the department as Deputy, and Bill Balfour, John Chadwick Jones and a few secretaries were the other staff: Betty Richards was Ken's secretary. Ken also started a day-release course for shop-stewards. I also gave some lectures for engineers, and taught foremen at Newport Tec.

So I took the train in from Rhiwbina to Newport Road, about four miles, and left B with her two toddlers. Later I got an old 50cc Honda, which was fine downhill with the wind behind. When we had to go to trade union meetings, or were out doing home interviews, which provided the main data of the research, I sometimes took our Cortina Estate.

B's luck was to have Hugh and Hoppy Davies next door, with a toddler Mark the same age as Chris. Hugh was doing psychiatry at Whitchurch, for a couple of years until he became a GP in Bristol – before the Severn Bridge was built. (We went over to see them on the day the Bridge opened, which was a very gridlocked day so a bad mistake.)

So Chris and Mark played together a lot. Chris called Mark "Boy", and referred to himself as "Doy", and so a new nickname was born. We had to get him an identical trike to Mark's one as otherwise he grabbed the trike. B and Hoppy got on famously: the Davies had a family chalet in Gwbert, near Cardigan, where we could go for weekends.

In summer B often went for the day to nearer beaches at Southerndown with her toddlers and others. Gilly Soper lived out near there.

Pat and Dick Barker, who had shared B's flat in London, were not far away, also with two young daughters. Ken Jones and Shirley had Bronwen and Mabbli, and later Evan, but were slightly further away in Cardiff. Malcolm Ballin was one of the company industrial relations people in the works we were studying, and with his wife Frances had 12 children I think, and then fostered more.

Jennifer and Gareth Bowen with sons Jeremy and Nicholas and daughter Bridget were also near. And Garfred and Cilla Congreve were in the psychology department and lived in the town centre. Oh, not to forget Jim and Liz Robinson, through whom we first met Cilla and Garfred. And Mike and Jan Harkness, lovely New Zealanders with two young girls.

B was kept busy with the two boys, and Joanna on the way. She had Jo at home, with Dr Gang standing by, but a midwife managing the birth, amazed at Jo's length (24 inches) so that she weighed her twice – 12 pounds. The children slept in one room, in two two-tiered bunk beds.

B once famously fell downstairs while carrying a cup of coffee – the resulting large brown stain on the wallpaper was there until we left.

We had a small garden, with a large wooden climbing frame and slide and sandpit in it. And a garden shed that I filled with newspapers from which I had not read everything. Peter thinks it harboured rats hiding underneath – huge ones, Chris adds.

The house was near the far end of a lovely peaceful cul-de-sac, so the young children were able to play outside, on their little tricycles and in small groups with their friends. A large mesh wire fence closed the end of the road from an idyllic burn in which the children caught tiddlers using butterfly nets and jam-jars, and there was a meadow of long grass and wild flowers beyond.

Bread and other groceries were offered by delivery vans which came down the street, and Chris remembers B's shouts from the kitchen as he helpfully raced from the bathroom – where he had been sitting with dreadful diarrhoea – to the front door to relieve the baker delivering bread.

B's shouts of "No, don't touch the bread!" changed to howls of pained frustration as the bread was discarded in the interests of hygiene, and Chris was sent back upstairs to wash his hands.

Another day Chris was one of a team of 3 naughty wee boys who came across the baker's van open and unattended (delivering to a front door no doubt), and they crept in and started putting grubby fingers into some very fancy cream buns; B bought the lot, and Chris was punished with a fierce reprimand combined with the knowledge that everyone else was enjoying the fruit of his naughtiness. The best punishments are never forgotten.

Chris first, then Pete later, started nursery school and then primary school in Cardiff. Pete did not want to be separated from his older brother on the first day, howling in tears when it was suggested that Chris had to go upstairs while he had to stay downstairs with a bunch of strangers.

On weekends we went for gentle hill walks, with bracken and mysterious dips where the boys would hide. They sent messages on notes up the string of our kite which flew magnificently in strong Welsh winds.

The research project was for one year, extended to two, and after that Ken went to work in London for the Post Office

Engineering Union, living in Maidenhead, while I stayed on for three more years as a temporary lecturer, doing research on white-collar unions in the steel industry.

B had discovered the pill, and we deliberately came off it to have our fourth child, Rebecca. After that I had the snip in a strange set-up: I think it was a private Catholic hospital, and a kind surgeon who did it under a local for nearly nothing.

B founded a baby-sitting group, based on sister Sue's model, where paper tokens were exchanged for hours of baby-sitting, so we were free to go out – there was a French restaurant in Tiger Bay called Elizabeth's that was a particular favourite.

One evening, while waiting for the baby-sitter, B dropped a bottle of meths which smashed, leaving a sea of liquid meths all over the kitchen floor. "What will I do?" she asked, so I said "Burn it off."

We often teased each other, so I watched calmly as she took some matches, lit one, and lit the meths, so that the floor became a sea of fire, moving under the kitchen cupboard and setting off other bottles with bangs and crashes. I stamped on it, and my shoes went on fire. We were both wondering "What do we tell the Fire Brigade?" when it luckily burnt out.

Once on our way back from staying with Hugh and Hoppy at Gwbert, we had suitcases on the roofrack. At some point we noticed from the flapping groundsheet that something was missing, and we had to backtrack to find that a case had blown off, and had been handed in to the nearest police station.

For me, it was amazing how B smoothly expanded her care from looking after me, to two boys, and then to four under-fives.

It was a time when we got free concentrated orange juice from the State for children under five, and once when I had to collect it, and asked for four, the staff member thought I was mistaken and told me off, turning to sympathy when I swore there really were four under-fives (for a few weeks after Becca was born).

Chapter Nine

Braeside: 1968-1985

I got a job at Heriot-Watt University as a full time lecturer in industrial psychology, initially based in the Grassmarket. When we looked for houses in Edinburgh, we didn't find any we liked or could afford. B went out to visit Braeside, in the little Fife village of Charlestown, and was charmed by it, the sun and the resident Ogilvies (and perhaps a sherry or two.).

So we bought it for about £9,800 and moved there. Braeside is a large detached house, made of sandstone, and standing on its own land of around three acres. It is at the foot of a steep, winding drive, and there's a fine view out on to the River Forth from the house – a literal stone's throw away.

Moving was tricky, as the removal people had to offload into a smaller van to get down the steep little hill, and it took a long time to get things sorted. Luckily the house was huge compared with where we had lived in Cardiff, and we gradually filled the big spaces.

The kitchen had a coal-fired Aga, and B thrived on this, learning to make bread and meringues, while I brewed beer and wine on the warm high shelves in the kitchen.

The coal was a bit of a dirty nuisance, and we converted the Aga to oil just in time for the 1973 oil price rise. There was a pulley in the kitchen for drying clothes. One time the rope broke, and it crashed down on my head, giving me the opportunity to feign serious injury and unconsciousness to give B a fright.

B made Braeside an incredibly welcoming warm house, and lots of friends visited. The kitchen was the cosy centre of it all, where people congregated. The phone on the wall behind the door was B's communication centre, and I had to install an extra long phone cord so that she could cook while she chatted. There was a small breakfast room off the kitchen, and this is where we had family meals.

It was furnished with a pine table and two pine benches, which I had made myself. The breakfast room was the centre of many family discussions (at one time, we used to have a weekly family "meeting", with minutes etc.) as well as incidents such as the one where B threw a bowlful of Instant Whip dessert over me and the breakfast room wall, after I'd dared her to do so. Jo remembers her own distress at the loss of her pudding course.

There were some outhouses outside the back door, and the washing machine and deep freeze were kept in one of these, next to the coal shed, with a lean-to greenhouse on the other side.

In a parallel house, also built about 1860, half a mile away, lived Isabelle and David Habib, who had Suzie and Maddy, roughly the same age as Jo and Bec. Isabelle and B became close friends, and were sometimes mistaken for each other – the only ladies in the village who wore jeans in those days.

We babysat for each other. David died of cancer at the age of 35, leaving Isabelle to cope on her own. She moved to a smaller house in Limekilns, and ended up moving on to Australia. B and Isabelle wrote detailed weekly letters to each other for many years. Pete stayed with Isabelle in Queensland on his gap year when he was 17, and Isabelle remains in contact today. She wrote:

"B and I were very similar heights and weights and used to dress (jeans of course!) very similarly. When the girls were small they would come hurtling into the house and throw themselves round the nearest pair of legs always convinced that the legs must belong to 'their' mum!

"Lots of the people in the village used to confuse B and me as we often had all four girls with us. B was SO amazingly good about looking after S. and M. when I was working, and they have great memories of happy times sitting round the table in the dining room while B appeared to feed multitudes with ease. She was also great at reading them stories, books they still remember well. Wind in the Willows was a favourite. I still cook many things from recipes that B made; pate, pork in cider, all sorts of soups.

"We used to iron together: a horrible job made much nicer by taking iron, and board, and a huge pile of clothes to each other's homes and sitting chatting while we ironed. B used to get in a great flap before she had to make a more formal meal for Z's University lecturers and used to want me to just go and sit and talk while she cooked, but most times she was "doing the flowers" which took her ages but looked so pretty, while I worried about the meal instead! She always got it done though. When she broke her arm on the ski slope in Edinburgh she couldn't do her hair so I used to go up and do it for her.

"We often swapped clothes especially long dresses for parties and dinners and thought it was great fun when people used to mix us up. B loved spring especially and got terribly excited when the first snowdrops appeared or a green sheen on the trees.

"Stays up at Nethybridge with picnics and gathering blueberries; and was it Chris who had his legs in plaster and we had to carry him everywhere?

"B is one of the most special people in my life and I think of her as the sister I never had. Every memory of our times together is special and I will always think of her with great affection."

All four children went to Limekilns Primary School 2 miles away. Bec called her 20 year old teacher, Sheila Walker, "Mummy". Mrs McLaren, the school lollipop crossing lady, knew everybody and was a tower of strength and Chair of the Community Council when it started. The school, and the pre-school playgroup, run by Chloe Dyer, helped us to integrate with other young families.

Braeside's land, with the woods and pond, were my escape, and eventually I hired a digger on a local building site to scrape out a circular pond and dump the mud in the middle as an island, which I planted with grass and willow trees. I kept ducks – Muscovies that Fenella gave us, and later Indian Runners and Rouens – and they produced new ducklings every spring. I set up a bowline for the kids to slide along, and there was always work to be done – cutting trees down, chopping up firewood, collecting driftwood from the shore. The boys helped as they grew up.

B's escape was the "bower": perhaps a wartime aeroplane-watching station, which I dug out and planted with grass and a few clematis. It faced south, and B loved to sunbathe there. She sunbathed topless, and indeed, she sometimes gardened topless too, which could cause some amusement. She had a wild free spirit inside her.

The garden around the house was more formal, with grass that needed to be cut regularly, a busy vegetable garden, and 187 roses in four beds that helped train the children that there are adverse prickly consequences to falling off a bike when you are learning to ride. B loved flowers, and the banks of snowdrops and daffodils in the woodlands around Braeside were the source of huge annual pleasure.

Fraser and Eleanor Anderson, with three boys, close in age to Chris and Pete, built a new house on the half of Braeside's land that the Ogilvies had sold off, and were lovely neighbours (although their boys were perhaps even wilder than ours). The middle boy, Phil, was a natural electronic genius; at the age of eleven, he rigged up a working phone line between his bedroom and Pete's at Braeside – a distance of 200 yards.

Kit and Graham Buckley moved, with two lovely daughters, from Limekilns to new houses built round the harbour at our back gate.

On B's 50th birthday I remember vividly that I invited a heap of her friends to a breakfast party, and as she lay on in bed, she heard singing in the hall below, and nakedly leaned over and suddenly found them. I think the McVeans and Bryants were there too.

The playgroup and the primary school were how we made most friends. But the adjacent villages of Charlestown and Limekilns were friendly places, and the local GP and his wife, George and Mary Hendry, did a lot to introduce new people like us to others. We went to church in Limekilns as a family every week which was another community builder. We used to go swimming as a family in the Royal Navy swimming pool at Rosyth. One time, on the way home, B skidded on ice on a sharp corner, in one of her very few road accidents.

We also got into having lodgers, 18 to 22 year old foreign language assistants working for a year at local secondary schools. They lived in our spare room, joining the family for meals and chat, each one staying for a year at a time. I try to list them below.

Monique has stayed in touch, and been over to see B recently. I remember when she first arrived with her parents; B managed in excellent French with them. Her boyfriend,

Angel, arrived soon afterwards, and Angel's friend Carlos too, for a short while. Barbara and Werner have recently been in touch again too. And Wolf Rozenzweig, now Mayor of a town beside Hamburg, visited us in summer 2011.

1971 Murielle
1972 Barbara and Werner
1973 Monique
1974 Wolf
1975 Didier
1976 Christine
1977 Joelle
1978 Klaus
1979 Christina. Detlief

B also had a penchant for collecting other waifs and strays. For example, Elspeth Maher moved in to live with us for a while, along with her Springer Spaniel, after her marriage had broken up. Years later, we had Monty living with us for some time, and I don't doubt that he needed help, but he was quite a handful. His hobby was "fighting", and he had a bunch of friends with similar inclinations. I gave him my old motorbike for painting a long fence, and he managed to wreck it in a very short time. At least one of his friends was killed in a motorbike accident.

We also took in George Russell's son, Chris, and his wife, who needed a refuge to get away from drugs. I don't think it really worked. George was an artistic man who gradually painted our large drawing room, and we stayed in touch with Ruth, his wife, a shoefitter, for some time after he died from lung cancer.

We gave Sam Craigen a home, while she collected some work experience in a Dunfermline hospital. This is surprising, when she had a medical grandfather-in-law in North Queensferry, but B was wonderfully welcoming and hospitable.

Like most families, we had strong traditions. We always had a traditional Sunday dinner with roast chicken, and for years, B's sister Fenella came out for the day. When Fenella moved out to Canada, B's parents Mary and John started to come out every week. They also came every Christmas for the traditional turkey dinner.

B also thrived on making Christmas decorations – red card hearts, inspired by Anne Lise, a Danish friend, and plaited straw and folded paper stars. She also made gingerbreads for a shop in Dunfermline for a while.

Pete remembers being in the drawing room at Braeside while she read The Hobbit to him. "I must have been about six years old. And I remember her coming to say goodnight when I was in bed after you both came back from being out for dinner - her scent was distinctive - Chanel No. 5 (was it?) combined with some G&T on her breath. And B on the phone in the kitchen in Braeside (Limekilns 238), with the extra long phone cord, and cooking on the Aga at the same time."

Jo remembers that when B made Christmas dresses for the girls, she used the remnants to make identical dresses for their Tiny Tears dolls, beautifully accurate with lace trimmings.

Joyce remembers the Christmas tree with real candles. We lit them and then continued on about our business and she spent the next 30 minutes stressing that the tree was going to catch fire. "You all seemed oblivious . . . and of course everything was fine. (My migraine mind took a while to recover.) I also remember the little gift she set at our places. And years later the little figures she would hang by the girls' beds when they would visit Edinburgh on holidays - thoughtful, thoughtful, lady.

"Gin and tonics were B's and my thing. She would often phone me when you were out and say she felt like a gin and tonic but didn't fancy one on her own. So we would both put the phone down, pour ourselves a careful measure, slice the lemon, splash on the tonic, pick the phone up again and spend a pleasant 20 minutes or so chatting.

"I always felt blessed to have such a lovely mother-in-law, because you do hear some terrible stories. B handed her son over graciously and generously. Having children of my own now I realise it isn't always easy to share your children.

"I loved B's 2CV. It was such a B car. It never seemed right to see her driving a 'normal' car once the 2CV's were taken out of production. I still get a real nostalgic twang on the very rare occasion I see one.

"B's soups are another lovely memory. Again the gin and tonic in the kitchen, chatting, laughing, relaxed, while B put together these wonderful soups, followed by dinner.

"We have a great picture taken of B and Anna in a playground years ago, with B stuck on top of the climbing frame, the only granny actively playing with her grandchild. We laughed so much that evening. It was the funniest thing. It took some time to get her back down to firm ground.

"Another time and indeed another experience captured on camera. We were in the Botanics feeding the squirrels with little Anna, when B discovered that she had a loose pair of tights captured in the leg of her jeans. She started to pull at them. She pulled and pulled and pulled and I laughed and laughed till I thought I would no longer be able to breathe."

Easter was another time for traditions. We boiled coloured eggs to roll down the hill in the garden. B made dye by boiling onion skins, and then put leaves inside a nylon stocking to dye a pattern on to the egg shell. The Cocky Ollie bird brought Easter Eggs for the children. One year, Flicka the dog ate Joanna's egg before she had found it.

We had several pets at Braeside. Sheba, the Golden Retriever, was the matriarch – arriving in 1969 and staying with us till her death at 15. She had pups, of which we kept one, Flicka, Jo's pet. The younger dog used to run off with Sheba often and it was only when Flicka was killed on the road that this problem stopped. Pete was given a cat – Honey – for his sixth birthday in 1968. It was only when she went in to be spayed that we realised that "she" was a "he". Pete also had a grass snake that escaped and was recaptured a few times.

B went back to work as a community midwife when Bec was about 6, I think, and zipped all over West Fife in her 2CV. She had done a refresher course, and then worked nights at the Western General with Judy Duck for a few months. She loved the work – mainly healthy happy mothers, where she felt useful. She was less happy with her managers, who didn't really understand the community side. She also drove the children fifteen miles to Dollar Academy every morning, once they all began to go there, as the early buses didn't coordinate well, although they used to catch the buses home (or hitchhiked to save the fare). She sometimes got through over snowdrifts when the public buses failed.

This was when B started teaching the children to cook, writing out recipes for them to manage when she was working over the weekends. Soups, simple but tasty main courses, and salads were learnt this way, and years later written into a notebook for Pete to take with him when he went to Australia for a year between leaving school and starting University. Later still, I collated them and published The Fledgling Cookbook, with several revised editions. It is still in daily use by me, and still selling.

At one time, when B's depression was making her indecisive, she asked the four children to write their favourite dishes on index cards, which she could then shuffle to decide on the next meals.

She also played squash a lot, with Charlie Smith who lived in Limekilns, among others, and for the Dunfermline Ladies' team, and with Helen Scott (Malcolm's wife). She was an unorthodox but fit and effective squash player. She had a lot of fun with Dave Paterson, the son of a local orthopaedic surgeon, who remembers teaching Bec to skate at Coylum Bridge where he had a winter job. Ian and Vicky Paterson also went to Limekilns church, where he was an elder, as I was.

B was also a brave skier, though we only had one foreign holiday (at Madesimo, Italy, in a hot April in 1974). Training for this at Hillend, the artificial ski slope south of Edinburgh, she saw Charlie Smith blow over in a gale. He broke his leg, and B skied down so fast after him that she did three somersaults and broke her right elbow and dislocated her left thumb, a week before Christmas. We also skied a lot from

Mountain View, B's family cottage outside Nethybridge, but skiing in the Cairngorms was usually more challenging than pleasant because of the wind and rain and cold.

B's parents and my own parents died during the 1980s and 1990s, while we were at Braeside. There were some difficult emotional times for us both.

B was a lovely mother, a natural with babies and toddlers. Teenagers were harder to handle, but she had a gift for high speed repartee that would get through to them. Our children describe our parenting style as "liberal" – our relationship with them was based on discussion, persuasion and trust rather than a disciplinarian, enforcement approach. Spankings were effective with Chris until around 10 or 11, when he was just too big, but his younger siblings usually backed down and escaped. Chris was never easy at that age.

As a young teenager, Pete remembers B looking at him steadily in both eyes, one hand on each of his shoulders, as she talked to him about the important things in life, such as the need to think of others, not to trifle with others' emotions, to be honest, truthful and reliable.

B and Z gave all four children a strong sense of their own self-worth, and as adults, they would all agree that they have an inner confidence that stemmed directly from the loving support given to them at all times by both B and Z.

We also gave the children considerable freedom from an early age. Each of the four children went to spend the summer with Fenella in Canada on their own when they were only 14. (Bec took a friend, Pamela, to make it less lonesome out there.)

Becca remembers when she and Joanna came back later than instructed from playing on Charlestown green, and sneaked up to bed, where B found them and spanked them. Jo's memory is that they locked themselves in the bathroom. B persuaded them to unlock the door and take a spank.

I don't think we spanked a lot, but sometimes it seemed important to make an impact. For example, Bec was only two when we moved there, and our back gate led straight to an unprotected railway line (one train a day shunting into the Crombie ammo depot) and below it a 75 degree slanting sea wall with the sea several feet deep at high tide. Bec was forbidden to go there but did, and had to be made aware that it was forbidden.

B was a gifted cook, with family favourites such as Moussaka, Tuna and Noodles (with carrot and pineapple jelly) as well as Z's special birthday meal of Beef Olives and Lemon Meringue Pie.

Chris, Pete, Jo and Becca remember their childhood years at Braeside as a time of freedom compared to the controlled lifestyles of children in the twenty first century. They played in the woods, camped out sometimes; the boys went shooting with air rifles, and times seemed care free. One time when we had the long steep driveway down to Braeside tarmacked, the truck ran over Pete's bicycle, causing irreparable damage.

Looking back, Chris realised with a shock that his own life had been incredibly blessed when visiting friends in their own homes; the huge amount of space at Braeside is something he still yearns for, and would love to pass on to his own children; a closer relationship with nature and the countryside.

Chapter Ten

Parties

Didier, one of the lodgers, had a party in 1975. The crowd of young people seemed quite controlled, so B and Z allowed Chris to have a party with his friends soon after. This was marred by smoking and drinking, with cigarette burns and drink spills on the carpets. B described it as a "fiasco".

The next teenage party took place in the outhouses which the children had decorated with graffiti and cartoon murals.

We also had several great parties of our own, spreading out into the garden when it was sunny. But more often B made anybody's arrival into a warm party, and when she was not there, it just was never the same.

Gavin's wife, Kate, remembers B as "beautiful, generous, vivacious: someone very special."

Chapter Eleven

Family Holidays

Our "standard holiday" was to Mountain View, B's parents' cottage near Nethy Bridge in Strathspey. We went at least twice a year, and have many happy memories of hill walks, golfing outings, blaeberry picking competitions, picnics at Feshie Bridge and games of cards in the evenings. B was very fast at Racing Demon, and Bec developed into a fierce and promising competitor.

Later, we sold Mountain View to B's cousin Rosemary, and had some wonderful holidays in sunny places like Greece and the Pyrenees. B was a great walker.

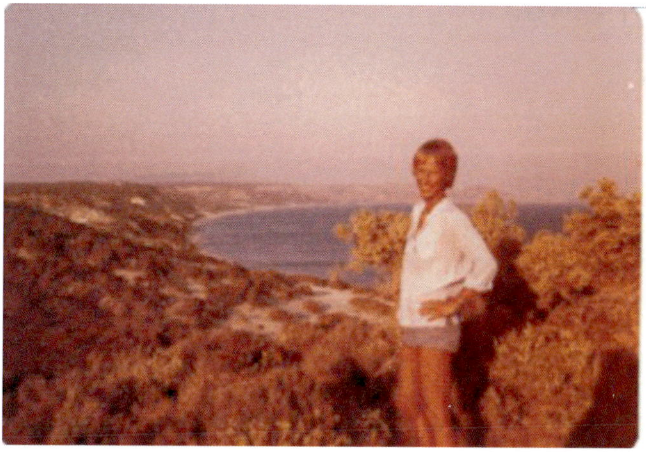

Chapter Twelve

B's style

B could have been a model for Laura Ashley. Her natural good looks combined with her sense of style would have been a perfect fit. She loved long, flowing shirts, neatly fitting long skirts and beautiful material. She had long, wavy brunette hair in her thirties, a brief frizzy Leo-Sayer-type perm in the early 80s, then short hair for most of the rest of her life.

Chapter Thirteen

Lennox Street 1985–

We thought of moving after Bec left school, and we, mainly B, sold Braeside well, to the Stephens, for about £100,000, which at x10 is not bad appreciation for 17 years. We lived for 9 months in Magdala Crescent, where Pixie Campbell's mother had recently lived and died. I think we looked at about 90 houses seriously, mostly on the South side, until B found Lennox Street, at an amazingly moderate price (£60,000), which left us with enough capital to knock it about a lot, and B's sense of style and flair came into its own again. Some of the changes she suggested to our builder Jeremy, like the door to the living room from the kitchen, and the door between the drawing-room and living room were inspired. It was just a shame that he went bust from owing VAT on previous jobs before the work was finished.

I haven't mentioned B's bipolar disorder. Her father had it, mainly depressed, and when she was about 40, B became severely clinically depressed. I won't write at length about it, as it is utterly miserable – like staring into a dark tunnel with no light at the end. B was off work, spent time in the Royal Ed., and eventually came through.

One positive outcome from depression was that she worked for a while on the Samaritans' telephone help-line. She made friends in a long-term way with some of the people she befriended there, and there is little doubt that first-hand knowledge of depression was an asset for the work.

Her manic attacks were far fewer, but caused far more havoc round her. There was a very memorable one, when we were staying in Magdala, and Zante had just had six puppies. B was put in a secure ward, after (during admission) swallowing a ring with a cross and a similar necklace. She smashed the "unbreakable" window with a drawer from her chest. I was left to feed and clean the puppies' mess, and sell them – not easy while working.

B recovered and was fine for a while, then she would deteriorate and need extra medical care again. She worked on, first at the City Hospital in an AIDS ward for a couple of years about 1990. This job showed her intense compassion for people in trouble, and outcasts. She did find it really hard to learn all the drugs in her first year, but she worked at it.

One of her colleagues there, Pauline, remembers two things about B. She was always radiantly cheerful; and at a time when there was no effective treatment for AIDS, that was wonderful. And sometimes she would go missing, and be found tending a terminal patient with her full attention. A lovely tribute.

She then moved to Croft Home Care, an agency started by Nonni Cobban, later Convenor of Alzheimers Scotland, to care for people living independently in their own homes. She loved this work and her patients and some of her colleagues too, in particular Jill Rock, with whom she nursed one wonderful old lady called Madge.

It was mainly getting clients up in the morning and putting them to bed at night, with some help with lunchtime meals occasionally. (It later seemed ironic in 2009 when B began to have helpers coming to help her bath and get dressed.) It's an important service, and B loved it. Strangely BNA and Healthcall who took over the business had a habit of texting B on her mobile on New Year's Eve saying they were desperately short of staff, for something like ten years after she stopped working.

She had to write a project, and chose to do it on "Little Things", something emphasised in Florence Nightingale's "Notes on nursing" and something that resonated in B's heart. Her care with little bunches of fresh flowers was somehow part of this.

She still played squash, and was in the Dean Ladies first team, and thoroughly enjoyed it. She could beat me on occasion, although she pointed out that if I began to lose, I hit the ball very hard to try and get back to winning.

In 1992 we both went to Australia where I had a sabbatical for six months in Woolongong. B had her best squash accident here, playing against Val Bamber, when she went after a drop shot and broke her wrist and raised a huge bump on her head.

B loved flowers, and seemed to be able to pick a bunch at any time of the year from our small garden. She enjoyed putting little bunches in the spare room, giving them to friends and neighbours, and to her patients, and often simply on the dining-room table. The rockery was her special thing.

Teresa remembers going with B to pick wild snowdrops at Cammo House. On one occasion, a patrol of park-keepers stopped them, and B was very contrite, but after some minutes, sneaked back and they filled their baskets.

She thoroughly enjoyed being a granny, "Granbee". After Bec and Conor and their children moved away from Edinburgh, she would send a hug down the phone to Cameron, with a "Whoooosssshhh."

Granbee pics on next page…

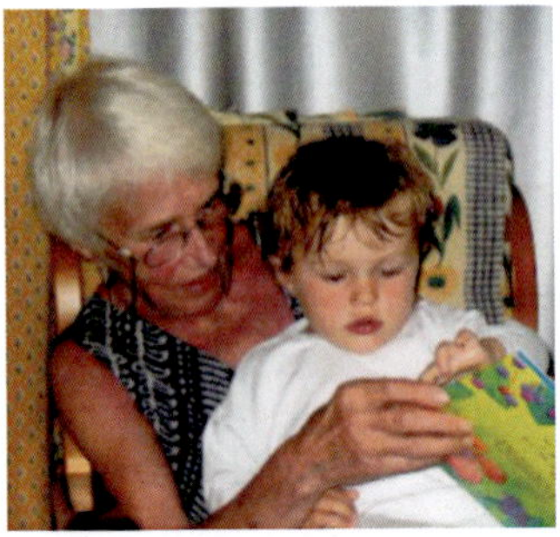

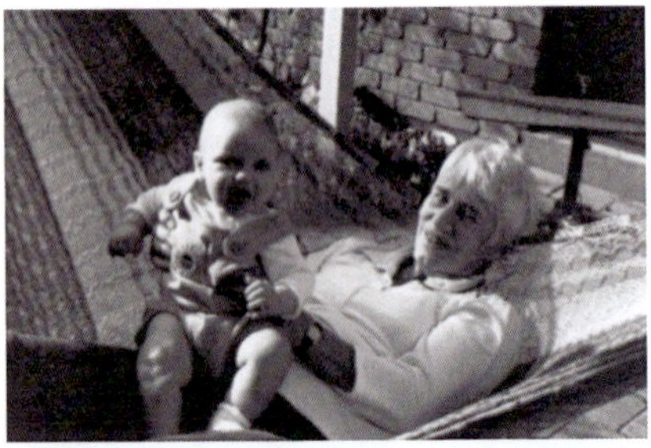

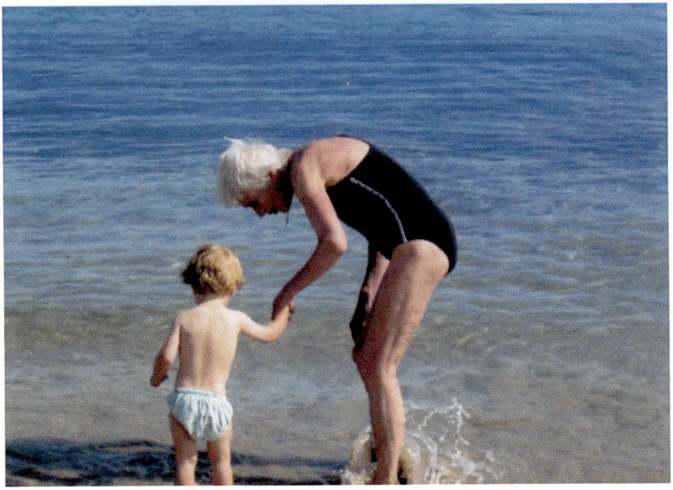

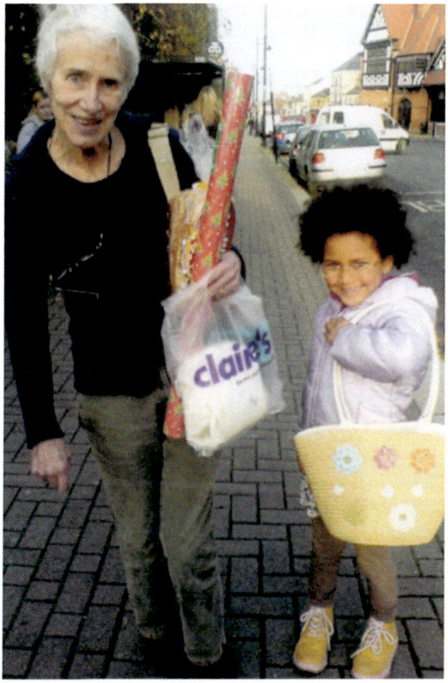

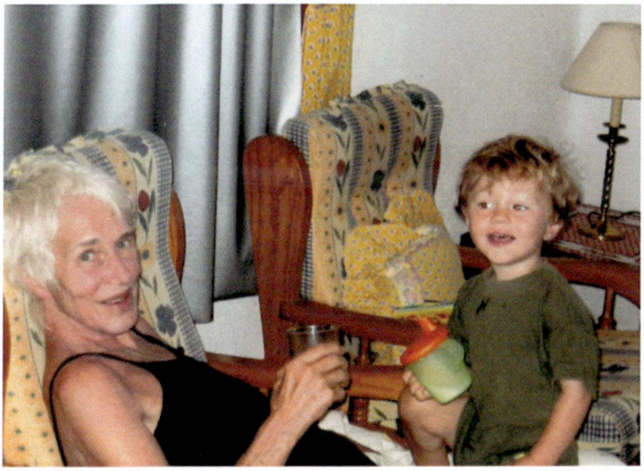

Chapter Fourteen

Perfection

B wasn't always perfect, and we did have points of friction. One silly one that I remember acutely was that she preferred to have the toilet paper hang down the back, and I preferred it down the front. So we would both switch it to the way we wanted it, without coming to an agreement. She was also talented at putting on silly faces like this.

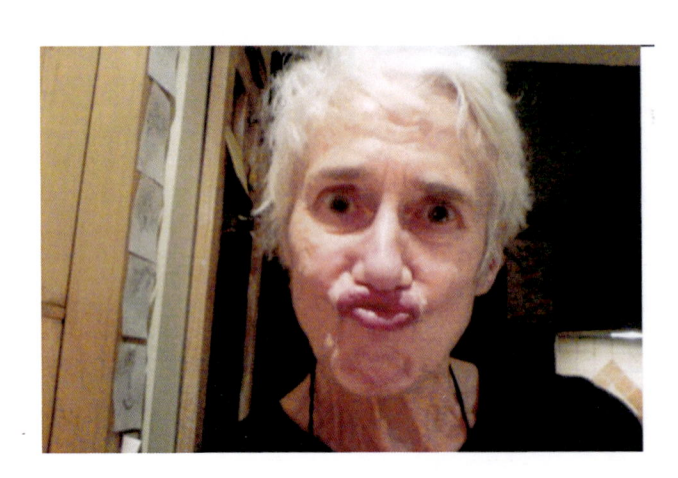

Chapter Fifteen

Alzheimer's Disease

B's Alzheimer's was first diagnosed by a psychologist in 2005 after some episodes of mild forgetfulness, and this was followed by a scan which showed large holes in her temporal and parietal lobes. Alzheimer's tangles the brain cells, and eventually destroys them. It is part of the wonderful flexibility of the brain that other parts can compensate for a while.

For a few years, it was just like extended absent mindedness, but she did fall a lot and cut herself, ending up in Minor Injuries or with the Practice Nurse to be patched up. She also occasionally felt shut in, and was rescued from wandering a few times by kind neighbours.

The council fixed up more banister rails, and a bath lift, and eventually somebody to come in 3 mornings a week to help to bathe her. She went into Pentland Hill care home on a trial basis on 24 November 2010, the day before the heavy prolonged snows started. Conor came up and helped to take her down to Manchester for that Christmas, and Peter even took her on a car run up around Arthur's Seat after that, but in about April 2011, she was deemed unsafe in a wheel chair, and became bedridden. Her bed is electrically adjustable, using a handset control– a very nice bed but a horrible life really, needing to be spoon-fed and given drinks with a straw.

She had always taken pride in her appearance, and still has a certain aura of greatness about her.

B was an April girl, and she gave me this rare serious poem by Ogden Nash for Christmas 1985.

Always marry an April girl

Praise the spells and bless the charms,
I found April in my arms.
April golden, April cloudy,
Gracious, cruel, tender, rowdy;
April soft in flowered languor
April cold with sudden anger,
Ever changing, ever true –
I love April. I love you.

Ogden Nash

From "Candy is Dandy: The Best of Ogden Nash", 1994, Carlton Books, André Deutsch Limited, 1994, reproduced by permission of Carlton Books Limited for UK printed rights, and for worldwide English language rights by Curtis Brown Ltd.